THINGS TO DO IN CHILDREN'S WORSHIP

BOOK 4

SUSAN SAYERS

Kevin Mayhew

First published in 2000 by
KEVIN MAYHEW LTD
Buxhall
Stowmarket
Suffolk IP14 3BW

© 2000 Kevin Mayhew Ltd

The right of Susan Sayers to be identified as the author
of this work has been asserted by her in accordance
with the Copyright, Designs and Patents Act 1988.

All rights reserved.
No part of this publication
may be reproduced, stored in a retrieval system,
or transmitted, in any form or by any means,
electronic, mechanical, photocopying, recording or otherwise,
without the prior written permission of the publisher.

Things To Do in Children's Worship, Book 4 is adapted from
Living Stones, Year B, by Susan Sayers, published by Kevin Mayhew Ltd, 1999.

0 1 2 3 4 5 6 7 8 9

ISBN 1 84003 536 6
Catalogue No 1500350

Cover design by Jonathan Stroulger
Edited by Peter Dainty
Typesetting by Louise Selfe
Printed in Great Britain

Foreword

In this book, I hope to provide material for use in children's worship which is helpful to those churches which do not follow a set programme of readings and themes. The material is arranged thematically, first in broad categories and then, by way of the indices at the back of the book, in a more detailed manner. When planning for children's work, it is advisable to read through the suggested Bible passages prayerfully. You are then in a better position to see how the programme relates to the theme, and also to supplement and vary the material as a result of your own insights and the specific needs of your group.

A few general ideas about storytelling:

- Tell the story from the viewpoint of the character in the situation. To create the time-machine effect, avoid eye contact as you slowly put on the appropriate cloth or cloak, and then make eye contact as you meet the children in character.
- Have an object with you which leads into the story – a water jug or lunch box, for instance.
- Walk the whole group through the story, so that they are physically moving from one place to another; and use all kinds of places, such as broom cupboards, under the stairs, outside under the trees, and so on. Needless to say, every care should be taken to ensure children's safety wherever you work with them.
- Collect some carpet tiles – blue and green – so that at story time the children can sit around the edge of these and help you position the cut-outs for the story.

May God bless you all, and the children with whom you worship.

SUSAN SAYERS

Acknowledgements

You are the King of glory, 1978, used by permission of Word's Spirit of Praise Music/CopyCare, PO Box 77, Hailsham, East Sussex, BN27 3EF.

My Lord, what love is this (verse 1 and chorus), 1989, used by permission of Make Way Music, PO Box 263, Croydon, CR9 5AP. All rights reserved. International copyright secured.

Contents

WHO IS JESUS?
    Descendant of David   8
    The Word of God   11
    The Messiah   12
    Light in Our Darkness   14
    He Joins Heaven and Earth   16
    The True Vine   17
    The Good Shepherd   18
    The Bread of Life   20

JESUS COMES AMONG US
    Ready for Jesus   24
    A Fresh Start   26
    The Shepherd King   28
    Wise Men Seek Jesus   30
    Jesus at a Wedding   32
    The Paralysed Man   34
    A Deaf Man Hears   36
    A Blind Man Sees   38
    The Rich Young Man   40
    Jesus' Ministry   42
    Calming the Storm   44
    Food for Five Thousand   46
    On the Mountain   48
    The King on the Donkey   50
    In the Temple   52
    The Cost of Love   54
    Jesus Is Alive   56
    Jesus and Thomas   58

THE CHRISTIAN LIFE
    Jesus' Family   62
    Jesus' Friends   64
    Hearing and Believing   66
    The Spirit Comes   68
    Loving Obedience   69
    True Greatness   70
    True Religion   72

Living Wisely	74
Trusting God in the Dark	76

God and Creation
The Mystery of God	78
The Spirit of God	80
Caring for Creation	82
God's Wonderful World	84

The Everlasting Kingdom
The Kingdom Grows	86
The End of the World	88
The Saints in Heaven	90
The Eternal King	91

Index of Uses
Topics	94
Bible Characters	95
Activities	95
Bible References	95

Who Is Jesus?

Descendant of David

Things to read 2 Samuel 7:1-11, 16
Luke 1:26-38

Things to do *Pass the ring.* Thread a ring on a length of string. Everyone holds the string, passing it through their hands. One person stands in the middle of the circle. The ring gets passed secretly along the string from hand to hand. The person in the middle has to try and guess where it has got to. When they are right someone else takes over in the centre. Finish by giving a pack of sweets to whoever is holding the ring, and asking them to hand the sweets round to everyone, so that as the ring is revealed, everyone is given a gift.

Explain that all through the hundreds of years before Jesus was born, God's promise had been passed on, from one generation to the next, sometimes seen and sometimes hidden from public view, until at the first Christmas, when Jesus the Christ was born, that message was seen clearly, and has been bringing blessing to everyone ever since.

But what was the message? Let's first go back in time to about 1000 BC – that's about three thousand years ago. We are in the city of Jerusalem, and this is King David.

1.

King David Hello, Nathan. I've been thinking.

Nathan Not too hard, I hope, your majesty.

King David I would like to build a fantastic temple for God to live in. The best temple ever for the best and only God. We all have nice houses to live in, but the ark of the Covenant is still in a tent.

Nathan Well, it sounds a very good idea, your majesty. Let me go and sleep on it and pray about it. See you tomorrow. Goodbye.

Narrator So Nathan went away and next day he was back.

King David Good morning, Nathan! What did God think of my idea?

Nathan	Well, it's a good idea and God is happy that you love him and worship him. But he is quite happy living in a tent and moving around with all of you. The temple can be built later on.
King David	Who will build it then?
Nathan	The temple will be built by your son, when he is king. But God has an important message for you.
King David	Really? What does he say?
Nathan	God wants you to know that he has planned a kingdom which will last for ever and ever. The King who will reign for ever will be from your own family. Long after your days are over, this King will bring joy to the whole world.
King David	Goodness, that's amazing. Excuse me, Nathan, I must go and say thank you to God for this.
Narrator	Hundreds of years later a woman was visited by an angel. The angel, whose name was Gabriel, told her she would have a rather special baby, and must call him Jesus, which means someone who saves or rescues.

2.

Gabriel	You are to call the child Jesus. He will be great and will be called the Son of the Most High. The Lord God will give him the throne of his father David, and he will reign over the house of Jacob for ever; his kingdom will never end.

(King David walks into the scene and says to the children sitting watching . . .)

King David	Hey, did you hear that? This woman is going to have the King that God promised would come! And this woman is engaged to Joseph, and he's from my family. So God was right. As usual. He's never lets you down, you know!

10 Who Is Jesus?

Gabriel	*(To King David)* Excuse me, but could I get on with my message to Mary, please?
King David	Oh, sure! Sorry to push into another time zone. I just got excited, that's all!
Mary	I am the Lord's servant. May it be to me as you have said.

Things to pray

Once in royal David's city
stood a lowly cattle shed,
where a mother laid her baby
in a manger for a bed.
Mary was that mother mild,
Jesus Christ her little child.

The Word of God

Things to read

Hebrews 1:1-3
John 1:1-5, 9-14

Things to do

Play a simplified game of 'Pictionary,' using a blackboard or sheets of lining paper fixed to the wall. Whisper the word to the first drawer and everyone shouts what they think it is. First to guess gets to draw next.

As we saw, it's sometimes quite hard to know what someone is thinking if you can't use words. Words make it much easier for us to understand one another. That's what they're for. Ask them to give instructions for getting to somewhere close by – their school, for instance, or a well-known shop – and to give a description of a familiar object.

God wanted all the people he had made to understand that he really loved them. He wanted them to understand what God was really like. If we were to look at the world God made, what could we tell about him? (Collect their ideas.) So we can tell that God is generous and loving, careful and thorough, clever and organised, gentle and powerful, just by looking at the world, because it expresses what God is like, just as words do. It was through God's Word that all this came to exist.

Now show some Christmas cards with Jesus as a baby on them. Eventually, God's Word was not just spoken but actually lived. Jesus is sometimes known as the Word of God, because his life expressed exactly what God is like – a living Word for us to understand in our human language!

Things to pray

Word of the Father,
now in flesh appearing!
O come, let us adore him,
Christ the Lord.

12 Who Is Jesus?

The Messiah

Things to read

Isaiah 61:1-4, 8-11
Luke 4:16-21

Things to do

The next object is . . . Have a number of objects hidden from view. Give out a short description of an item, such as: 'This object is black and white and re(a)d.' The children raise their hand when the item matching the description is shown. Show several other items before showing a newspaper, which fits the description, even though it may be slightly different from what was expected. Here are some other ideas:

- The next object has a face all the time (a clock)
- The next object is for the heads of li(e)rs (a pillow)
- The next object is to play with when you get round to it (a ball)
- The next object is put up at the down times (an umbrella)

Talk about how we knew what to look out for in that game, so we could recognise the object when it appeared. And sometimes we understood the description better after we'd seen the object.

Today we are looking at some of the things the prophets said to describe the coming Messiah, long before Jesus was born. When Jesus did appear on earth, those things came true, and people found they understood them better than they had before.

On a large sheet of coloured paper, draw an outline of Jesus, his arms stretched out in welcome, based on the picture below, and lay this on the floor. On top of it have a sheet of the same size but different colour, which has been cut into sections. On each section have written out the different sections of Isaiah's prophecy. Across all these lay a title on white paper which says 'Messiah' on one side and 'Christ' on the reverse. It should all look like this:

Tell the good news to the poor	Comfort the broken-hearted
Set free those feeling imprisoned	Announce the time when God would show his merciful judgement
Give people clothes of praise and joy to replace their sadness	Be fair to everyone
Make what is right grow strong	Put wrong things right

MESSIAH

Explain how the prophets were sent by God to prepare the people for the coming of his chosen one. The Hebrew word for this anointed, chosen person was 'Messiah'. The Greek word was 'Christ'. (Turn the title over and back as you say this. Leave it on the Messiah side.) As the Old Testament is written in Hebrew, we'll stick with their word, Messiah, while they are waiting for him to come.

In order to help the people get ready, God spoke through the prophets to tell them what the Messiah would be like when he came. That way they could recognise him, and be ready for him. Let's look at some of the things they said about this Messiah. Lay the Messiah title at the side, and look at the sections, one by one, with all the readers reading them out. In turn take each section off and lay them all around the emerging picture. Gradually we can see that all these descriptions fit the Jesus we know from the Gospels. And as the New Testament was written in Greek, we'll use the Greek word for him: the Christ. (Reverse the title.)

Things to pray

Jesus, Jesus, we have come to see
that you must really be
the Son of God our Father.
We've been with you and we all agree
that only in your service
can the world be truly free!

Light in Our Darkness

Things to read

Ephesians 5:8-14
Revelation 12:1-5a
John 3:18-21

Things to do

Make the room as dark as possible, and have a powerful torch. The children start at one end of the room and try to creep up to you without you seeing them moving in the light of the torch, which you sweep like a searchlight slowly back and forth across the room. Anyone caught moving in the light has to come and help you check for other movers.

Flash the torch around again and talk together about how light shows up things which are hidden in the darkness. When might we be pleased to have the light spotting us? (If we were shipwrecked and wanting to be rescued; if we were lost in a dark wood; if we're doing something we're proud of; if we're dressed in our coolest clothes.) When might we not want the light to spot us and show us up? (If we're doing something we know we shouldn't be doing; if we're wearing something awful; if we're up to no good.) The thing about light is that it can't help showing everything up clearly, both the good and the bad. Shine a torch into a dark cupboard and it might show up either a ten pound note or a dead mouse the cat has brought in!

When Jesus went about on earth, God's glory couldn't help shining out of him and lighting up people's souls to them, so they saw themselves clearly, as they really were. God's light showed up to them very clearly all their nastiness and sin, as well as all their loveliness and goodness. That wasn't always a very nice feeling. People who were behaving badly, but pretended they were behaving well, found Jesus' light showing up their lies and they hated it. People who longed to live well, but knew they weren't very good at it, found Jesus' light showing them hope and forgiveness, and so they loved the light.

God's light still shines. It still shows up to us our nastiness and sin, as well as our loveliness and goodness. How are we going to feel about that?

If we were to hate everything good, honest and right, then we would do our best to shut God's light out, so the evil in us could be safely hidden to fester and grow in darkness again. But if we see God's light as a way of helping the goodness and honesty in us to grow tall and strong, we'll be very happy to let it shine in us.

Things to pray

All-seeing God, all-knowing God,
shine in my heart,
so that the goodness grows strong
and no evil can take root.

He Joins Heaven and Earth

Things to read Genesis 28:10-17
John 1:43-51

Things to do As a group build a bridge from newspaper. Get everyone rolling sheets of newspaper into firm sticks and fixing them together in a way that is strongest. (As far as possible, let the ideas come from the children, giving hints and nudges where necessary.)

Why do we build bridges? When there's something which blocks you off from where you want to be, like a river or a railway, a bridge over it will let you get there and back easily. Bridges join places and people. They fill the gaps between people or places. To work properly, a bridge has to be touching both ends.

Place down two squares with a space between them. One square is covered with red dots and has the word 'Us' written in black on it. The other is covered with green dots and has the word 'God' written on it.

God is so holy and almighty that it is impossible for us to see God and live, so he is hidden from us. If we want to know what God is like, where can we look? We can look at the world around us, at people, and at the Bible. But if we really want to see clearly, in a way we can understand, what God is like, there is someone who is like a bridge, bridging the gap and making it possible for us to be in touch with the holy, hidden God.

Lay down between the squares and touching them a long rectangle which is covered in a mixture of red and green dots, and has the name 'Jesus' written on it. Jesus is both God and human, so when we choose to follow him he is able to show us clearly what God is like.

Things to pray He came down to earth from heaven,
who is God and Lord of all,
and his shelter was a stable,
and his cradle was a stall;
with the humble, poor and lowly,
lived on earth our Saviour holy.

The True Vine

Things to read

Galatians 5:22-25
John 15:1-8

Things to do

Grow a vine. As children come in, tie a length of green string or wool round their waist, so it hangs down the back like a tail. Leave one child (or a leader) with no string and sit that person on a chair. When everyone is ready, explain that they are going to make themselves into a grapevine, using all the children. It has to start from the person on the chair, who has two hands free, and they have to obey this rule: one string to one hand. (It's good training for children to practise organising themselves like this, sometimes. Don't interfere unless it's really necessary and let them work through the mistakes to the solution.) Give out grapes to everyone when they're ready.

Bring along (or take them outside to see) a growing plant. Notice how its branches have grown, rather like we grew our 'grapevine', and notice any buds or flowers which are the first signs of fruit. Also look at an off-cut from the plant. Will this piece be able to flower and fruit like the other branches? No, it won't. Why not? Talk together about how the branches and stems carry all the goodness, and without being joined on to the living plant, with its strong roots, the cut-off branch dies.

Have a grapevine outline drawn on a large sheet of paper. Now, from a suitable translation of the Bible, read today's Gospel, where Jesus talks of himself as the true vine, and the importance of us being joined to him if we are going to produce fruit. Talk over what Jesus means, and what kind of fruit we are hoping to produce. As different ideas are given, stick clusters of grapes on to the drawn vine, labelling them. (They may well link up with the ones Paul describes in Galatians 5:22.)

Things to pray

Jesus, I know I can only produce good fruit
if I'm connected to you, the true vine.
Let your life flow into me and through me
so together we can make a huge harvest!
Amen.

The Good Shepherd

Things to read

Psalm 23
John 10:11-16

Things to do

To the rescue! Firefighters, lifeboat crews and mountain rescue teams are all willing to drop what they're doing and race to the rescue. At one corner of the room have a hose pipe, at another have a length of rope (or a washing line), and at another a blow-up ring on a length of string. Everyone walks about in the space in the middle of the room until one of three alarms is sounded. If it's a bell they race to the sea rescue, and all line up holding the string, hauling the ring in. If it's a whistle they race to the mountain rescue, and all line up and walk along a pretend narrow ledge, holding the rope. If it's a 'nee-nor' siren (just voicing it is fine) they race to the fire rescue, and line up to hold the hose, directing it at the flames.

It takes courage to join any of those rescue teams, and those who do it know that they may be putting themselves at risk, but they are willing to do it so that others will be saved.

It was a risky, dangerous business for Jesus to rescue the human race, using only the power of love. In today's Gospel Jesus talks about himself as the Good Shepherd, who is willing even to lay down his life for the sheep. We're going to look at what it means to be a good shepherd, so that we can better understand what Jesus meant.

Have most of the children as sheep, some as wolves and bears, one as a hired shepherd, who's only doing it for the money, and one as a good shepherd who loves the sheep. Talk the sheep through their life on the hillside, with the good shepherd watching that they don't get lost, finding them tasty pastures full of wet, juicy grass to munch, leading them to drink at the water, and getting them safely into a pen (made of chairs) for the night. The shepherd lies down in the doorway to sleep. Meanwhile the wolves and bears stand back, howling and waiting for a chance to catch a sheep. If they start to come near, the shepherd throws crumpled paper 'stones' at them and that frightens them off.

Stop the action and swap shepherds. This shepherd reads the newspaper instead of checking that the sheep have enough to eat and drink, and he's listening to his personal stereo so he can't hear the sheep bleating when they're frightened. If a wolf comes near, he might throw a stone or two, but the wolves know that it's worth waiting, as he'll soon lose interest. When he gets deep into his *Goosebumps* book, some of the wolves creep nearer and are just about to grab a sheep. The shepherd sees the wolves and runs away! That kind of shepherd is no good for the sheep. That kind of leader is no good for God's people.

So when Jesus says that he is the Good Shepherd, we know what he means – that he loves us and looks after us, even if it turns difficult and dangerous; even if it costs him his life.

Things to pray

Jesus, we thank you that you were willing
even to lay down your life for us.
May the love which saved us
live in us every day and for ever.
Amen.

The Bread of Life

Things to read

Exodus 16:2-4, 9-15
John 6:24-35

Things to do

Beforehand draw pictures of several different meals (or cut pictures from magazines). Cut these into wedge-shaped servings and scatter them all around the room. The children find the separate pieces and put them together so they end up with complete meals.

Look at the different kinds of meals we have made, and at the variety we like to eat during the week and during each day. If we put all the things we ate in a week together, it would be quite a lot, and even though we feel nice and satisfied just after we've eaten breakfast, we're still looking forward to lunch by the end of the morning and tea by the evening.

God has provided us with a rich planet to live on which has plenty of food for us to eat – there's enough for everyone if only we were better at sharing. We use the fruits, roots and vegetables that grow in it, and the animals, birds and fish that live there. God has provided wonderfully for our bodies.

Remind the children of the time when Jesus fed that huge crowd of five thousand people with bread and fish. That was a different kind of feeding in a way, because Jesus was looking after them spiritually as well as physically. The next day after that the people went out searching for Jesus again. They had been very impressed by all that bread and fish and they were hoping for some more.

But Jesus said, 'Don't just run after the kind of food that satisfies the body. The body won't last for ever – some time it will die. A much better idea is to run after the kind of bread which will feed you spiritually, so that you'll stay spiritually alive and healthy, even after you're dead.'

So the people thought that sounded the best kind of bread, but they didn't know how to get hold of it. They'd never seen any in the baker's. They said to Jesus, 'Give us this kind of bread, sir. We'd like to live on that bread which gives life which lasts for ever.'

Then Jesus looked round at them and said, 'My Father has given you the true bread from heaven to give life to the world, and it's standing right here in front of you. It's me! I am the bread that gives you life!'

Jesus meant that just as ordinary bread is very good at satisfying us and keeping us physically alive and healthy, so Jesus himself is the one we need to believe in and be with for spiritual life which goes on whether we're still alive here or whether our bodies have worn out and died. In Jesus we can go on being very much alive for ever, just as Jesus is.

Things to pray

Jesus, I know that you were born as a baby,
lived and worked among us,
showing us God's love,
that you died on the cross and rose again to life.
I know you are alive for ever
and I want to stay close to you
right through this life
and on into heaven. Amen.

Jesus Comes Among Us

Jesus Comes Among Us

Ready for Jesus

Things to read
Isaiah 9:6-7
Mark 13:24-27, 32-37

Things to do
Get ready to . . . Each time the children crouch in the 'get ready' position, and when you show a symbol of a particular activity, they have to mime it until the whistle blows for the 'stop and get ready' stage again. (Possible items might be a football, tennis racket, swimwear and goggles, a horse shoe and a paintbox.)

Prepare the signs and symbols below to be placed on the floor during the teaching.

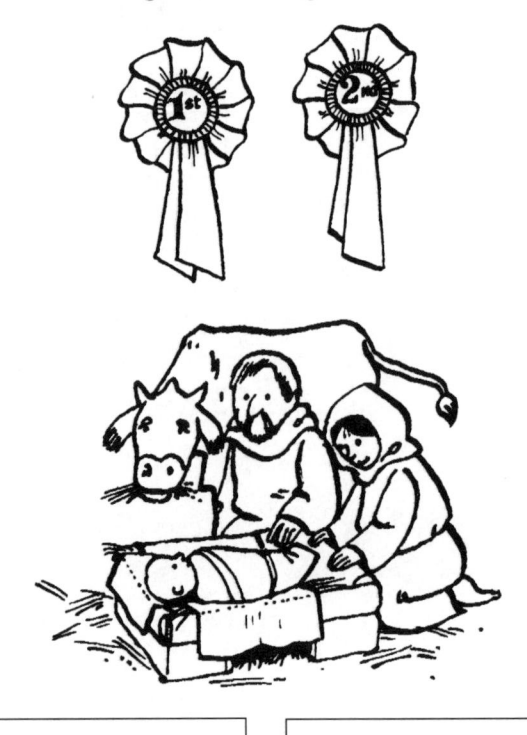

Explain that Advent means 'coming' and the person we're waiting and preparing for is Jesus. Now place down the '1st' rosette as you tell them about the first time Jesus came to earth. (Involve them and use what they already know.) As you discuss that first coming, place down the picture of the Nativity.

As you display the '2nd' rosette, tell them that the manger at Bethlehem wasn't the only time for Jesus to come to our earth. We are told in the Bible, by the prophets and by Jesus himself, that he will be coming again one day. Place down the 'When?', 'Where?', and 'How?' cards, and read excerpts from today's Gospel to find out the clues we have been given. Go over these in discussion, displaying the big question mark as you draw the clues together and establish that there is still lots we don't know (and even Jesus didn't know) about exact times and dates. What we do know is that it will happen, and we need to make sure we keep ourselves alert, so that we'll be ready for Jesus when he comes in glory.

Things to pray

Jesus, get us ready to meet you
when you come again in glory,
so that we can welcome you
when we see you face to face.

A Fresh Start

Things to read

Isaiah 40:1-5
Mark 1:1-8

Things to do

What's different? Get into pairs. Take it in turns for one to hide their eyes while the other changes something about the way they are standing or what they are wearing. See if the difference is recognised, then swap roles. Ideas for differences: cross arms in different way, hair tucked behind other ear, shoelace undone/done up, ring on different finger.

Sometimes we don't notice things that we are used to seeing. Today we are going to look at someone who got people noticing things they had stopped looking at. (Have two people in conversation for this.)

What was his name?
His name was John. One day no one had heard of him and the next, there he was out in the wild desert outside Jerusalem, drawing huge crowds of people because of what he was saying. They felt he was telling them what they knew they needed to hear. They didn't come because what he said was easy – in fact, it was very challenging – but he made them feel they wanted to go for it with everything they had.

Go for what?
Sorting their lives out. They started to look closely at how they were really thinking and behaving – John helped them notice their own bad habits and the unloving, discontented way they were living. They suddenly wanted to put those things right. John told them it was like road-building.

Road-building?
Yes. He said they needed to build their lives like a good road ready for God to come to them, a road that was straight and true with no mountains of greed or empty pits of cruelty and grumbling. And they needed to start building it straightaway.

Why?
Because John said it wouldn't be very long before God's Messiah was coming to live among them, and they all wanted to be ready for that.

So what did they do about their road-building?
Well, like I said, they had a good look at themselves, saw what needed to be changed, told God about it and then John washed them.

Washed them?
Yes, they waded into the local Jordan river, and when they confessed their sins John dipped them right under the water as a sign that their lives were being washed clean.

That's a good idea. You'd really feel you were making a fresh clean start if you were dipped right under water in a flowing river. Now they would feel they'd done what they could to be ready for the Messiah.
Yes, that's right. And we can do the same, you know.

We can?
Oh, yes. If we take a look at how we speak to people, and what we do for them, and what we don't do for them, we'll soon see which bits of our road need changing. Then we can tell God we've noticed them and are sorry.

What will God do?
He'll forgive us and give us a fresh start.

Perhaps we could do that in the bath or shower?
Good idea.

Things to pray

Loving God, open my eyes to see
what needs changing and putting right
in my thinking, speaking and doing,
because I want to turn away from sin
and turn towards you.
Amen.

Jesus Comes Among Us

The Shepherd King

Things to read

Psalm 78:70-72
Luke 2:8-20

Things to do

Play 'Simon says' but make it 'King David says'.

Remind the children of when King David lived (about one thousand years before Jesus, which is about three thousand years ago). One way of doing this is placing four bricks spread out in a line across the whole floor as thousand year markers. Walk with the children from the first brick (which you can label 'King David' as you pass it) on to the second thousand years marker (labelled 'Jesus Christ') on to the third (labelled 'Battle of Hastings') until they reach the last marker (labelled 'Now!').

Dress one child as a shepherd boy. When David was a child, his job was to be out with the sheep in the fields near Bethlehem, looking after them (everyone makes bleating noises), keeping them safe from wolves and bears (wolves howling and bears growling), and leading them to the places where there was plenty of grass to eat, and water to drink (sheep eating and drinking noises).

A thousand years later, when Jesus was born, there were still shepherds in the fields near Bethlehem, looking after their sheep (bleating noises), keeping them safe from wolves and bears (wolves howling and bears growling), and leading them to the places where there was plenty of grass to eat and water to drink (sheep eating and drinking noises). As you know, Joseph was from King David's family, and that's why Joseph and Mary had come to David's home city of Bethlehem for the register. And, as you know, Jesus was born while they were there.

The angels could have told anyone about the birth of this baby, couldn't they? But who did they tell? It was the shepherds in the fields near Bethlehem, while they were at work, looking after their sheep, keeping them safe from wolves and bears, and leading them to the places where there was plenty of grass to eat and water to drink (appropriate noises).

When we read that the shepherds were the first to be told about the baby Jesus, it reminds us that:

Jesus Comes Among Us

1. Jesus grew up to be like a good shepherd, because he looks after us all, keeps us safe from evil, and leads us to where we can be spiritually fed and watered. (Place down a woolly lamb and a crook.)
2. Jesus is a 'son of David', born in David's city and of David's line, or family. (Place down a family tree with Luke's genealogy on it, showing David clearly at the top and Jesus at the bottom.)
3. Like David, Jesus is a King, not just for a while in history, but for ever. (Place down a crown.)

Things to pray

Jesus, born in David's city
born of David's line,
you are my shepherd
and you are my King.

Wise Men Seek Jesus

Things to read Isaiah 60:1-6
Matthew 2:1-12

Things to do Sit in a circle, passing a locked box round to each in turn. As each one holds the box they say, 'One day I would love to go to . . . and see . . .' This can be a place or a person, a thing or an event, anywhere in the world or the universe. (Start it off yourself so they get the idea.)

Share something or somewhere you had always hoped to see and which was different but even better than you had expected when you actually got to visit it. Today we are learning about some people who found what they were hoping to find, but it was all a bit different from what they expected.

Have everyone kneeling back on their heels, as in 'Do you want to go on a lion hunt', slapping their thighs with their hands to make the walking noise.

The children just repeat what you say.

Chorus
We're going on a journey . . .
a very long journey . . .
far away from home . . .
We're looking for a king.

We've noticed a star . . . *(point up)*
a very big star . . . *(look up, screwing up eyes)*
and we know it means a king!
Hold on! . . . We've come to a river . . .
Let's wade across . . . Swish, swish, swish.

Chorus

Hold on! . . . We've come to a mountain . . .
Let's climb over it . . .
   (do slow slaps up it and fast down the other side)

Chorus

We stopped at a palace . . . *(stop the 'walking')*
a very fine palace . . . *(bow to the ground)*
but there was no new king. *(shake head)*
Herod didn't know anything! *(shrug shoulders)*

Chorus

The star led us to Bethlehem . . . *(stop the walking)*
it led us to a house . . . *(point forward)*
a very ordinary house . . .
> *(a 'can this be the right place' look!)*
and we knocked at the door . . . *(clap three times)*

Chorus (changed to 'We've been on a journey')

And he's here!
We gave him our presents
> *(carefully place gift on floor in front of you)*
We bowed in worship *(bow to the ground)*
He wasn't in a palace . . .
> *(resume the thigh slapping and shake head)*
He isn't rich at all . . . *(shake head again)*
But he's king of the mountains and rivers . . .
> *(speed up the thigh slapping)*
and king of us all!
> *(fast drumming on thighs, finishing with applause)*

Things to pray

We bring you the GOLD
of our obedience.
Help us to live as you want us to.

We bring you the FRANKINCENSE
of our worship.
You are God and we worship you.

We bring you the MYRRH
of our world's sadness.
Help us look after one another better.
Amen.

Jesus at a Wedding

Things to read

Revelation 19:5-9
John 2:1-11

Things to do

Sit in a circle. The first person says, 'I went to a wedding and I saw . . .' and names one thing or person they saw. The next person repeats the sentence, adding another thing of their own, and so on around the circle.

There are sound effects for the story today. Give a couple of children a bowl with water in it and two small pots. At appropriate times they can scoop up water and pour it out again. Give some other children instruments to play. Two children have wine glasses to clink as they say, 'Cheers!' At the asterisks, the children make the appropriate sounds.

Mary and Jesus and Jesus' friends were all invited to a wedding in Cana, which is a town in Galilee. When they got there the wedding music was playing cheerfully *. All the guests were chatting and laughing together *. There was plenty of delicious food to eat * and wine to drink *.

But then a terrible thing happened* (gasp). They ran out of wine * (gasp). Mary went and whispered to Jesus * and then she whispered to the servants *, telling them to do whatever Jesus told them to. Mary knew that Jesus would be able to help.

Jesus told the servants to fill the water pots with water, and the servants did as he said *. The wedding music continued to play cheerfully *. All the guests went on chatting and laughing *. None of them knew what the servants were doing. Then Jesus told the servants to go to the chief guest and pour out some of the water as wine, and they did as Jesus said *. He clinked glasses with his friends * and drank the water. But it wasn't water any more, it was top quality wine! * (gasp). It was the best wine he had ever tasted * (gasp). As the wedding music played on * and the guests chatted and laughed *, Mary and Jesus' friends and the servants smiled. This was the first of Jesus' miracles, and they had just seen it happen. (Everyone claps.)

Things to pray

Lord Jesus,
whenever we don't know what to do
or how to cope,
remind us to listen to you
and do whatever you tell us to.

The Paralysed Man

Things to read

Psalm 51:1-17
Mark 2:1-12

Things to do

Simon says. Point out that Simon is the only one with authority to tell us what to do.

Act out the story of the paralysed man, with most children being the crowd, and a couple being scribes. The four friends climbing the outside stairs and making a hole in the roof is done with sound effects, and everyone looks up and follows the (imaginary) man's journey down to the floor. Give the scribes their thought bubble card so they can read it out, and give Jesus his speech bubble card. Then gather in a circle.

> Your sins are forgiven!
>
> Why does this man say that? Only God can forgive sins.
>
> Stand up, take your mat and walk!

Place the thought and speech bubbles in the centre of the group, and read the scribes' thoughts out again. Explain that forgiveness means drowning someone's sins in perfect goodness and love, so only someone who is perfect in goodness and love can do it.

Were the scribes right in thinking that only God can forgive sins? Yes, they were. (You could read the children verse 25 from Isaiah 43, where God is speaking, through his prophet.)

Now look at what Jesus said. Why was Jesus able to forgive the man's sins? Because he really was God's Son.

Things to pray

Jesus Christ,
we have come to see
that you must really be
the Son of God our Father.
You love as the Father loves
and you forgive as the Father forgives.

A Deaf Man Hears

Things to read

Isaiah 29:17-21
Mark 7:31-37

Things to do

Give out some instruments for some of the children to play and ask the others to close and open their ears so they can feel what it is like to be shut off from the sounds. Swap the instruments around so the others can have a go.

Today we are going to hear about someone who couldn't hear anything at all, and he couldn't speak either. When he was trying to listen to someone, this is what it sounded like: (mime the words, but let no sound come out). Sometimes he could tell that people wanted him to do something but it was hard to work out what. (Mime the words 'please can you get me a chair' several times, getting more irritated as no one gets it, gradually adding gestures to help them understand.) People helped him as much as they could but it still felt very lonely being unable to hear. Sometimes he would see people saying something to each other and laughing, but he didn't get the joke as he couldn't hear the words. He hoped they weren't laughing about him.

One day his family said to him: (only mime the words) 'We're taking you to Jesus. He can make your ears better.' (Say it several times with increasing actions till they work it out.) The man was very pleased. He had seen Jesus before and thought he looked kind. Of course he hadn't been able to hear what Jesus had been saying but he had seen how interested the crowds were and how carefully they listened. He had even seen Jesus put his hands on people with eyes and legs that didn't work, and watched them shouting and laughing as they were made better. He could hardly wait to go to Jesus himself.

His family took him to where Jesus was, pushed through the crowd and said to Jesus (mime it only), 'Please, Jesus . . . put your hands . . . on him and make his ears better.' The man saw them speaking and worked out what they were saying, just as you have done. He watched Jesus nod and look straight at him, smiling. The man smiled back and tried to say, 'Hello, Jesus', but he couldn't speak so just some sounds came out. Jesus led the man away from all the people to be with him on his own. The man watched as Jesus put his fingers into the man's ears. He could feel them there but couldn't hear anything, like we usually do. Then Jesus spat and touched the man's tongue. Doctors at that time quite often used saliva in healing so to them this was quite an ordinary thing to do.

Now the really exciting bit happened. The man watched Jesus looking up to heaven and praying (mime only), 'Be opened! Be opened! Be opened!' Suddenly the man realised he had just *heard* what Jesus was saying, as well as *seen* what he said! He could hear everything, and a very noisy world it was, too. He could hear the birds all screeching and singing, the crowd in the distance, the leaves rattling in the wind and everything. The man started to say, 'Oh good heavens, I can hear!' And suddenly he heard his own voice speaking. Jesus had healed his speaking as well!

Things to pray

Father God, we want to pray
for all the people who can't hear properly.
We pray for those who are working to mend their hearing and making hearing aids to help them hear better.
Amen.

A Blind Man Sees

Things to read

Isaiah 42:5-7
Mark 10:46-52

Things to do

Blindfold everybody and stand them all over the room. Ask everyone to move about, and, when they find someone else, to hold hands and go on together, till they find someone else to join up with. When you can see that everyone is joined up together, tell everyone to freeze and open their eyes. They will be surprised to find that they are all linked up.

We are all going to act today's Gospel. Get to know the Gospel account really well, so that you can narrate it, directing various children to do the actions as they happen.

Put up a sign which says 'To Jericho' and choose someone to be Bartimaeus. Direct them to sit by the roadside and give them a begging bowl to hold. Bartimaeus is blindfolded. Choose someone to be Jesus and two others to be disciples. Gather the crowd at Jericho and explain that we are all following Jesus, who has been teaching and healing in the town.

All the crowd are walking on the spot. We're just leaving the city, and Bartimaeus can hear us coming, so he's shouting out at the top of his voice, 'Jesus, son of David, have mercy on me!' Now a few people are going ahead, trying to make the blind man be quiet. But the man is shouting even louder, the same thing again. This time Jesus stops, and we all stop as well. Jesus tells the disciples to call the blind man. They go over to him and cheer him up, telling him that Jesus is calling him. The blind man jumps up, not bothering to pick up his cloak, and comes across to Jesus. (The disciples might well be guiding him.)

Jesus says to Bartimaeus, 'What do you want me to do for you?' Bartimaeus says to Jesus, 'Teacher, I want to see.' Jesus says to him, 'Go, your faith has healed you,' and suddenly the man finds he can see. (Jesus helps him to take off the blindfold.) The crowd moves off down the road, very happy for the man, and Bartimaeus is walking with Jesus, looking around at things for the first time ever.

Things to pray

Jesus, you made the blind to see,
open my eyes to see your love.
Jesus, you made the deaf to hear,
open my ears to hear your truth.
All we need we find in you;
your love is total, your words are true.

The Rich Young Man

Things to read   Mark 10:17-31

Things to do   Today we're going to hear about someone who was seeking God for all he was worth.

You will need two of the leaders, two of the young people, or a leader and a rehearsed child to prepare this script. The actors can be dressed up.

(Jesus walks into the room and the young man runs up to him, kneeling before him.)

Young man   Good Teacher, what must I do to get eternal life?

(Jesus looks thoughtful, looks at the man, and helps him up.)

Jesus   Why are you calling me good?

(Young man looks puzzled.)

Jesus   No one is good, only God. You know the commandments? *(Young man nods, pleased, and counts them on his fingers as Jesus says them.)* Don't murder, don't commit adultery, don't steal, don't lie, don't cheat . . . *(The man looks puzzled again as this isn't one of the commandments.)* honour your father and mother . . .

Young man   Yes, teacher, I know all that. I've been keeping the commandments since I was a little boy! But I still feel I'm missing out somewhere. It's more than just obeying the rules, isn't it?

(Jesus looks at him and smiles, placing his hands on the young man's shoulders.)

Jesus   Yes, you're right, my son, there is more. There's something else you need to do – but it won't be easy for you. *(The young man looks pleased and ready to do anything. Jesus stands back and looks at him very seriously.)* Go and sell whatever you own and give it to the poor. All the treasure you have then will be treasure in heaven. Oh and then . . . *(Jesus smiles)* come and follow me!

Young man	*(Half to himself)* Sell everything . . . EVERYTHING! Oh my goodness. *(His face clouds over and he looks at Jesus, shaking his head in disbelief before walking away, muttering to himself.)*
	(Jesus turns towards the disciples, shaking his head sadly.)
Jesus	Oh dear, he's so attached to all the things he owns, you see. Do you realise how difficult it is to enter God's kingdom? Especially if you're used to having lots of nice things around you. I reckon it's easier for a camel to get through the eye of a needle than for the rich to get into God's kingdom.
Disciple	Goodness, Jesus, in that case who has any chance at all of entering the kingdom of God?
Jesus	*(Shrugs)* Well, if you're talking about getting into God's kingdom all by yourself, I'd say no one has any chance at all! *(He smiles)* But if you let God do it in you – that's a very different matter. The impossible becomes possible!
Disciple	But some people give up everything to follow you, Jesus.
Jesus	*(Nods)* That's right. And I can assure you that no one who sacrifices house, family or friends or land because of me will ever lose out. They'll get it all back many times over, in a different way, with eternal life thrown in!

Things to pray

It's so hard to enter the kingdom of God
but I want so much to do it;
harder than threading a camel through a needle,
but I want so much to be there.
Your kingdom of love and joy and peace
is the place I want to be,
and I know that only through God my Saviour
can I enter it and be free!
Amen.

Jesus' Ministry

Things to read

Isaiah 61:1-2
Mark 6:30-34, 53-56

Things to do

Have a clock face and arrange with the children that when it says 7 o'clock it's time to get up, 9 o'clock it's working time at school, 12 o'clock it's lunchtime, 4 o'clock is watching television, and at midnight everyone is fast asleep. When the clock time is displayed and called out, they do the appropriate actions.

Beforehand prepare a blue sheet to look like a motorway sign for services, based on the picture below.

You will also need a 30 mph sign and a sign for a carpenter's shop, together with a few wood-working tools and bits of wood, and a pair of sandals.

Begin by sharing a couple of different typical days from the group, one child and one adult, starting at waking-up time and going through to bedtime. Today we are going to take a look at a typical day in the life of Jesus during the years of his ministry.

Jesus grew up helping Joseph in the carpentry business the family owned. (Place down the carpenter's sign, the wood and the tools.) When he was grown-up he carried on working as a carpenter, sawing wood, hammering in nails, measuring, sanding down and polishing. During this time he lived at home, probably eating with the rest of his family in the evening after work.

When he reached the age of thirty (place down the 30 mph sign) things changed. Jesus stopped being a carpenter (pack the tools and wood away) and started the work God needed him to do among the people. Instead of living at home and being sure of a bed to sleep on and food to eat, Jesus set out walking around the country (place down the sandals), staying with friends, or sleeping rough.

(Now refer to the service station sign.) Jesus ate and drank wherever he and his disciples were invited, and whatever they were given. Sometimes this would be grand parties at the houses of rich, important people, sometimes they might be crowded into poor people's homes, laughing and talking late into the night, and sometimes they might go hungry. Sometimes they would stay for a few days or a few weeks with people, and sometimes there wouldn't be any shelter provided. Jesus once said, 'Foxes have holes and the birds have their nests but the Son of Man has nowhere to lay his head.' They never knew for certain in the morning where they might be that evening as Jesus just went where he sensed God wanted him to go. For transport they used feet, walking along the roads and tracks between the towns and villages.

So what was the work Jesus was doing for these two or three years? There were people who needed healing and comforting, forgiving and setting free from evil spirits. There were people living in the darkness of evil who needed to have God's light brought into their lives. There was lots to tell people about God so they understood how lovely he was, and there was the work of helping people learn to love one another and help one another. All of this was like the job of a shepherd – caring for the people and guiding them wisely.

And if we had lived in one of the towns or villages around the lake of Galilee at that time – nearly two thousand years ago, we'd have met Jesus; perhaps he would have eaten with us, or stayed at our house, or healed one of our friends, or played with us.

Things to pray

Be with us in the morning –
from the first yawn to the coco pops.
Be with us in school –
from 2+2 till the last full stop.
Be with us in the evening –
from the children's programmes till bedtime.
Be with us while we sleep –
from starlight to the new day's dawn.
Amen.

Calming the Storm

Things to read Psalm 107:23-32
Mark 4:35-41

Things to do Sit everyone in a circle on chairs. You are going to create a storm with actions and sounds. Each 'round', the leader starts off a new action, the person on the right joins in and so on around the circle. When it gets to the leader again, a new action is started. It's important that people carry on with the previous action until the person next to them changes – that makes for a gradual build-up instead of a sudden change. Here are the 'rounds':
1. Flick fingers, so they brush against one another (both hands at once).
2. Tap lightly with two fingers on the palm of other hand.
3. Clap lightly with fingers on palm.
4. Clap fast and louder.
5. Slap thighs with hands – left hand, right hand alternately and quickly.
6. Stamp with feet on the floor.
7. Still stamping, clap while you make wind noises.

(Then work your way back through the numbers to a calm.)

Our story today is about a sudden storm, rather like the one we've just made, so we're well practised for providing all the sound effects for it.

Jesus had spent all day out in the open air telling stories, and teaching and healing people. He used to sit in one of the boats to talk, with the water lapping * the odd fly buzzing around * and all the crowds sitting quietly on the beach. That way they could all see Jesus and hear him, and he could see them. But now it was evening, and there was Jesus sitting in the boat with the water lapping * and he was really tired *. All the crowds had crunched their way home along the beach *.

So he said to his followers, 'Come with me across the lake'. They waded into the water *, pushed the boat further out * and clambered aboard *. They felt which way the wind was blowing by licking a finger and holding it up * and then hoisted the sail *.

Soon they were moving through the water, with the waves making a wash behind them *. Jesus lay down with his head on a pillow in the bottom of the boat and fell asleep *.

But then the wind started to whip up strongly * and that made the waves bigger and higher, crashing around the boat *. The water started to trickle in over the side of the boat * and they had to pull down the sail *. The disciples were getting frightened. 'Oh my goodness, this is terrible! Our boat is going to be completely swamped!' they shouted. They were scooping the water out as best they could, but the wind was still howling * and the sea was still churning and rolling all around and all over the boat *.

Then they noticed that Jesus was still fast asleep in the bottom of the boat! 'Wake up, Jesus', they said, shaking him, 'Do you care about us or not? We're going to drown soon if this weather goes on.'

Jesus woke up, looked at his friends, and saw the fear in their eyes. He heard the sounds of the angry wind * and the boiling, churning waves (*** above the next part of the story). He stood up in the boat and commanded the wind and waves to stop – he called out to them: 'Quiet! Be still!' * Then the wind stopped and the lake became calm, lapping gently around them again *.

Jesus looked round at his disciples. They were completely stunned by what they had just seen. Who could this Jesus be if he could even take charge of the wind and waves? It was frightening to see such power in action.

Jesus said to them, 'Why are you afraid? Do you still have no faith?'

And they didn't really know what to say to him. One thing they had realised – that Jesus must be something more than an ordinary teacher – it was as if he had God's power.

They hoisted the sail again *, bailed out the rest of the water *, and sailed over the calm lake, with the water lapping the bow.

Things to pray

Jesus, we see in you
the power and love of God.
When we are like stormy water,
calm us down.
When we are frightened
and panicking,
give us your peace,
we pray.

Jesus Comes Among Us

Food for Five Thousand

Things to read

2 Kings 4:42-44
John 6:1-15

Things to do

Teach the children the song *5000+ hungry folk* with actions as shown below.

5 0 0 0+ hungry folk,
(five fingers on one hand, make ring with other hand which is shown three times, then rub tummies)

came 4 2 listen 2 Jesus. *(cup hand to ear)*

The 6 x 2 said O O O,
(use fingers for each number and for the O)

where can we get some food from?
(shrug shoulders and open hands, moving head from side to side)

Just 1 had 1 2 3 4 5, *(use fingers)*

loaves and 1 2 fishes. *(count with fingers)*

When Jesus blessed the 5 + 2
(hands face down as if blessing; count with fingers)

they were increased many x over.
(roly-poly with hands going upwards)

5 0 0 0+ 8 it up, *(use fingers, then pretend to eat)*

with 1 2 3 4 5 6 7 8 9 10 11 12 basketfuls left over.
(count on fingers and stamp each foot for 11 and 12)

(Ian Smale
© Copyright 1985 Kingsway's Thankyou Music)

Beforehand prepare some pieces of card or paper with questions on one side and the Bible references on the other. Arrange them question side up over a picture of the feeding of the crowd, based on the drawing opposite.
 Here are the questions and references for finding the answers:

1. What lake did Jesus sail over? John 6:1
2. What time of year was it? John 6:4
3. What did Jesus say to Philip? John 6:5
4. What did Philip reply? John 6:7
5. What food did the boy offer? John 6:9

Jesus Comes Among Us 47

6. What did Jesus tell the people to do? John 6:10
7. How many people were there? John 6:10
8. What two things did Jesus do with the food? John 6:11
9. What happened to the food left over? John 6:12-13
10. What did this miracle make the people want to do? John 6:15

Give out Bibles and help everyone to find John chapter 6. Then as each question is asked, the children can tell the story, checking with the Bible as they go. As each question is answered, take it off the picture and lay it at the side, until you are left with the whole picture and the whole story revealed.

Things to pray

Loving Father,
thank you for feeding us
with food for our bodies and our souls,
making us strong
so we can live good, loving lives.
Amen.

On the Mountain

Things to read

Exodus 24:9-18
Mark 9:2-9

Things to do

Climb a mountain on the spot. Everyone finds a space, and we all set off walking (on the spot) towards the high mountain. We stop and shade our eyes from the sun as we look up at the top in the distance; *that's* where we're going! As we go on it gets steeper . . . and steeper . . . and steeper . . . till we're struggling to walk upright. Soon we have to use our hands as well as our feet. Now we come to a high cliff face. We look up at it towering over us, and feel the cold rock with our hands. We'll have to be very careful, and find a hold for our right hand . . . then our left . . . then pull up on our feet and quickly find a new handhold . . . and another . . . as we make our way up the cliff face. When we climb over on to the top we've got to walk along a really narrow ledge. We flatten our hands against the rock to steady us, and move slowly along the narrow ledge. At last it starts to broaden out, and we're nearly at the top. It's not too steep, here, and we run the last bit to reach the very top of the mountain. Now we can stand on top of the world and look right down to the tiny path where we started off, far, far below. We can see far into the distance every way we look. (They can stay at the top, do the journey down again, or abseil down, and look back at what they've achieved.)

Everyone lies face in arms on the floor, as we imagine a rather different kind of mountain experience. Play some quiet music and lead the children in imagination on that walk up the mountain with Jesus, Peter, James and John, imagining it yourself as you speak, so that it rings true. Think of what you might see and hear and feel.

Things to pray

Holy, most holy, all holy the Lord,
in power and wisdom for ever adored!
The earth and the heavens are full of your love;
our joyful hosannas re-echo above!

(From the 'Slane Sanctus' by Michael Forster
© 1995 Kevin Mayhew Ltd.)

Jesus Comes Among Us 49

Holy, most holy, all holy the Lord

Holy, most holy, all holy the Lord, in power and wisdom for ever adored! The earth and the heavens are full of your love; our joyful hosannas re-echo above!

Capo 1 D G D
A G D G
D G D Bm G D

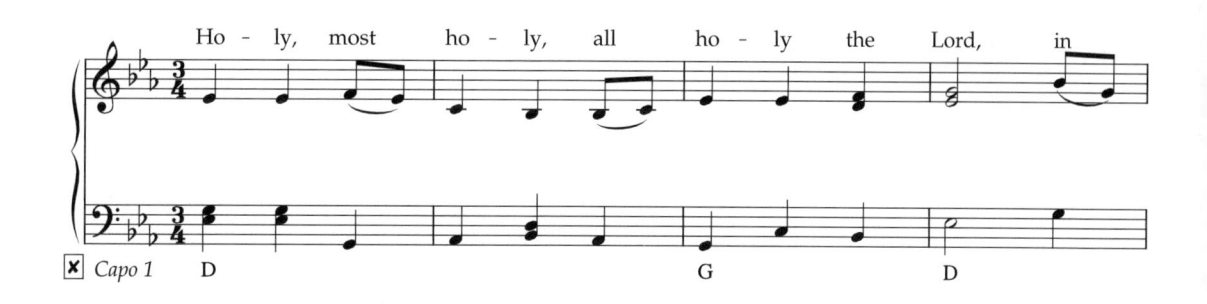

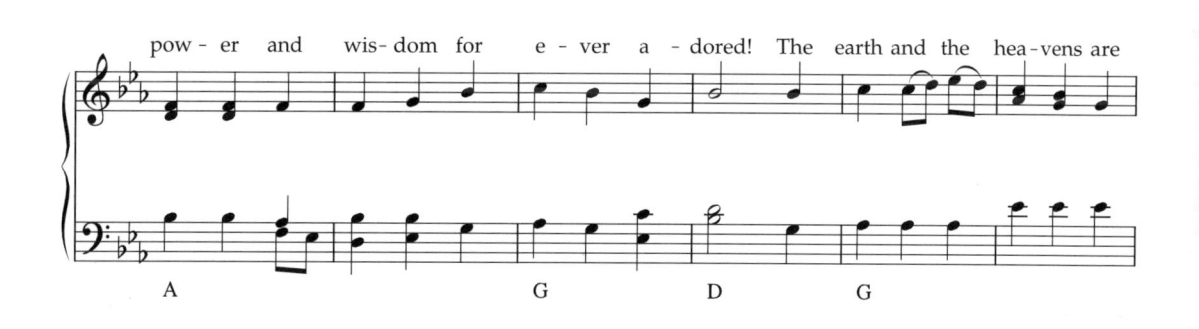

Words: Michael Forster. Music: traditional Irish melody, arr. Alan Ridout
Text and this arrangement © Copyright 1995 Kevin Mayhew Ltd

The King on the Donkey

Things to read

1 Samuel 16:1-13
Zechariah 9:9
Mark 11:1-11

Things to do

Gather all the children and take them on a Palm Sunday procession, preferably outside. Take a portable tape player so they can all sing along with the songs.

Bring along a little olive oil and a cloth, a crown, and this notice: 'Anointed as God's chosen one = Messiah (in Hebrew) = Christ (in Greek).'

Put the notice, the olive oil and the crown in the centre, and remind the children of when David was a shepherd boy and God chose him to be the future king. To show he was chosen (choose a volunteering child), David was anointed with olive oil. (Pour a little oil on the volunteer's head and wipe it with the towel, so they understand what being anointed means.) David was God's chosen king, and when he grew up, he became the king of Israel. (Place the crown on the same child's head.)

Long after King David had died, everyone looked back to those wonderful days when he had been their king, and they also looked forward to the time when God would send his anointed, chosen One to be King over all the world for ever. They knew this anointed one would be from King David's family. They called this anointed One the Hebrew for 'anointed' – which is 'Messiah'. We usually call it 'Christ' which is the same thing in Greek, the language the Gospels were written in.

Many, many years later, Jesus was born, of David's family. Gradually people began to realise that this was the Messiah, the son of King David who would reign for ever. When Jesus rode a donkey into Jerusalem, they all got really excited, and cheered and shouted and sang their hearts out. The prophets had even said the Messiah would enter Jerusalem riding on a donkey, and here Jesus was, doing it! 'Hosanna! Hosanna!' they all shouted. 'Hosanna to the Son of King David! Hosanna for the glorious kingdom he's going to bring us!' (One of the leaders can be a donkey and one of the children can ride the donkey while the others all shout their Hosannas and wave their streamers.)

What the people didn't quite understand was that Jesus' kingdom was not like a country on a map, but was a kingdom of love, joy and peace in people's hearts and lives. Jesus is the Christ, the Messiah, and reigns as King in our hearts now, just as he can reign in the hearts of anyone, living anywhere, at any time.

Things to pray

You are the King of Glory,
you are the Prince of Peace,
you are the Lord of heaven and earth,
you're the Son of righteousness.
Angels bow down before you,
worship and adore,
for you have the words of eternal life,
you are Jesus Christ the Lord.
Hosanna to the Son of David!
Hosanna to the King of kings!
Glory in the highest heaven,
for Jesus the Messiah reigns!

(Mavis Ford
© 1978 Word's Spirit of Praise Music/CopyCare)

In the Temple

Things to read   Isaiah 56:6-8
Mark 11:15-19

Things to do   An emptying and filling activity. Give each two or three children a small pot full of dried peas, a jug of water and two straws. To prevent spillage, put these on trays, fixing the pot of peas to the tray with a piece of blutack. The aim is to fill the pot with water, but to do this they first have to empty it of peas, using the straw-sucking method to pick up one pea at a time and drop it on the tray.

Point out that we couldn't fill the pots with water at first because they were full up with peas; we had to empty the pot before we could fill it as we wanted. Today we are going to hear about a whole building which needed to be emptied before it could be filled!

Find Isaiah 56 verse 7 in the Bible, and also have it written out clearly so everyone can read it together: 'My temple will be called a house of prayer.' Explain that what God wanted was that the whole temple would be filled with prayer, so that people could go to it and feel close to God there. The temple, at Jerusalem, was to be a very special place.

But when Jesus came to the temple at Jerusalem, he found that instead of being filled with prayer it was filled with a whole lot of other things. People were bustling about buying and selling; money was clattering at the money-changing desks, tradesmen called out their bargains; there were sheep bleating, pigeons cooing, and cattle mooing. What a racket! Give different children different noises to make (coins can be shaken in a pot) and orchestrate all the noise of the temple.

Jesus knew that this was the last thing the temple was meant to be like, because God had said (everyone joins in), 'My temple will be called a house of prayer.' There was only one thing to do; the temple had to be emptied of all this cheating and buying and selling so it could be filled with prayer as it was meant to be.

As God's Son, Jesus strode into all the noise and started upending the tables so all the coins went flying (do this with a couple of tables as you speak), and overturning the boxes and baskets, driving out all the people who were using the temple of God as a market place. And as he walked about, he shouted to the people, 'It is written, "My temple will be called a house of prayer", but you have made it a den of thieves!'

All the people were shocked and a bit scared. They knew Jesus was right. They knew they had filled the temple up with wrong things. But now it was empty, and ready to be filled with prayer, as God intended it to be.

Things to pray

Jesus, my life is filled with lots of thoughts,
lots of words and lots of activities.
Please show me which of them are good
and which are not,
so I can be like God's temple,
empty of anything wrong
and filled with your love.

The Cost of Love

Things to read

1 Peter 2:21-25
John 12:20-33

Things to do

Forfeits. Sit in a circle and spin a tray in the middle, calling out someone's name. That person tries to catch the tray before it clatters to the ground. If they fail, they have to pay a forfeit. Ideas for forfeits: count from ten (or twenty) back to zero; hop round the outside of the circle; give one of your hairs; blow up a balloon; wear a hat for the rest of the game.

One of the helpers (or a primed child) produces a tube of Rolos which has only one sweet left in it. You notice it and beg to have it as you love Rolos. The Rolo owner lays it on thick that this is their pack of Rolos, and they saved up all their pocket money to buy them. It's an awful lot to expect them to give up. Go on begging, reminding them of how nice you are and how much you mean to them. Eventually they say, 'Oh, OK – I suppose you're worth it!' and give you their last Rolo. Everyone else can say, 'Aah!'

Explain that today we shall think about what it cost Jesus to do his work as our Saviour. (Place a cross down on the floor in the middle of the circle.) It's one thing to dedicate your life to teaching and healing, wandering around the country with no definite place to stay, and working long hours without pay. Jesus had been doing that for the last two or three years.

But now things were taking a new turn. He knew that it wouldn't be long before his work of loving people to freedom led him straight into trouble, trouble that would be bound to end in giving up his life in a tortured, shaming death on the Roman gallows. (Raise the cross to standing and hold it there.)

Not surprisingly, Jesus shuddered at the thought of having to go through all that. It wouldn't just be the physical pain, either. It would mean taking on himself the whole terrible load of the world's sin and evil, and going on loving and forgiving to the very end. (Cover the cross with a purple cloth.) Everything human in Jesus cried out against having to do that. The cost was so great and so demanding.

But then he remembered that the whole point of

Jesus Comes Among Us

him being on earth was that he had come to save the people he loved. And to Jesus we are worth all the suffering. (Uncover the cross.) So today we remember that Jesus was prepared to say, 'Yes!' because he loves us that much.

Things to pray

My Lord, what love is this,
that pays so dearly,
that I, the guilty one, may go free!
Amazing love, O what sacrifice,
the Son of God given for me.
My debt he pays and my death he dies,
that I might live.

(Taken from the song *Amazing love* by Graham Kendrick © 1989 Make Way Music)

56 Jesus Comes Among Us

Jesus Is Alive

Things to read

Acts 2:22-24, 36-38
Luke 24:36b-48

Things to do

Take the children on a scary 'lion hunt'.

For the teaching today, write out the separate speeches, and give them to different people to say during the telling of the story. These are:
- Jesus: 'Peace be with you!'
- Various disciples: 'Help! It must be a ghost!' 'Aah!' 'A g-g-ghost!'
- Jesus: 'Why are you so scared? I'm not a ghost! Look at my hands and my feet. It's me, Jesus! Touch me if you like. You can see I have a living body. A ghost does not have a body like this!'
- Various disciples: 'Oh Jesus, you're alive!' 'Yes, I can see you are real. That's incredible!' 'Yippee! Jesus is alive!'
- All together: 'Are you REALLY alive, Jesus? It seems too good to be true!'
- Jesus: 'Do you have any food here?'
- One disciple: 'Yes, there's some cooked fish. Here you are.'
- Jesus: 'Thanks!'
- Various disciples (whisper): 'Look, he's eating.' 'Ghosts don't eat normal food!' 'He MUST be alive!'

Give out the speeches and imagine you are all in the room where Jesus came. Narrate the events, with the characters reading their parts. Then go on to tell them how Jesus helped them understand what had been happening. Hold a Bible and flick through the Old Testament as you explain that he took them through all the things that had been written about him in the prophets and the Psalms.
- Jesus: 'It is written that the Christ would be killed and rise from death on the third day. You saw these things happen – you are witnesses.'
- Various disciples: 'Yes, that's true, we saw it all happen.' 'Yes, we did.' 'We know it's true.'
- Jesus: 'You must tell people to change their hearts and lives. If they do this, their sins will be forgiven.'

- One disciple: 'OK, Jesus, we'll tell them. Where do we start?'
- Jesus: 'You must start in Jerusalem and then preach these things in my name to all nations.'

Pray together for all the people who will only hear about Jesus' forgiveness because we tell them during our lifetimes.

Things to pray

Dear Jesus, when we are scared you make us brave,
when we are worried you calm us down,
and when we are listening you tell us what to do.
Help us to listen well and tell others about you,
so they can enjoy your friendship as well.

Jesus and Thomas

Things to read

1 John 1:1-4
John 20:19-29

Things to do

Try again. Stand in a circle with one person in the centre. They throw a beanbag or soft ball to each person in turn. If someone misses a catch, they are given a second chance (or as many as it takes!).

Sometimes we are given just one chance to get something right, and if we mess it up that time, there are no second chances. Share some examples, such as music exams, writing in ink rather than pencil, answering a question on a quiz show, converting a try, or entering a colouring competition. Sometimes we feel like kicking ourselves afterwards and would love to put the clock back, so we could do it again, but differently.

Today we're going to hear about someone who missed out, but was given a second chance.

Have everyone (apart from one who is going to be Thomas) sitting on chairs, and one extra chair left free. Have an unlit candle in the centre. Remind them about Jesus rising from death on the first Easter Day, and explain that he came to where the disciples were gathered on that Sunday evening. They had locked the door because they were scared. (Rattle a bunch of keys.) As they can see, one place is empty. That's Thomas's place, and for some reason, which we don't know, Thomas wasn't there that evening. Perhaps he was so upset about Jesus dying that he wanted to be by himself.

Suddenly (light the candle) there was Jesus in the room with them. Once they'd got over their fear and astonishment, they were all very happy to see him, real and alive! Then Jesus left them just as quietly as he had come. (Blow out the candle.) But what about Thomas?

Well, during the week the disciples told Thomas what had happened, and Thomas couldn't really believe it. It was just too good to be true. And he said, 'Unless I see him with my own eyes, and touch his wounds, I refuse to believe it.'

A week later, the disciples are all together again, and this time Thomas is there as well. Once again Jesus suddenly appeared among them, without a fuss – he was just there! (Light the candle.) And because Jesus understood what Thomas had been going through, he went straight to him. 'Here I am, Thomas,' he said. 'Here are the wounds in my hands and side and feet. It's really me! Do you want to touch my wounds to make sure?'

Thomas didn't need that kind of proof any more. The experience of Jesus' presence was good enough – now, he *knew* it was true, and Jesus really was risen from the dead.

Things to pray

Dear Jesus,
when Thomas had his questions and his doubts
you met him and helped him to see the truth.
We pray for all those who have questions and doubts.
May they soon discover how real you are. Amen.

The Christian Life

Jesus' Family

Things to read

Romans 8:28-30
Mark 3:20-35

Things to do

Play happy families. Give out the cards equally. The children go round swapping cards until they end up with complete family sets. (You can either give a time limit or continue till all sets are complete.)

The people in our own families are special to us. Sometimes we have good times together, sometimes the people in our families make us cross and we make them cross. But people in a family are bound together closely because we are physically related to each other. We often look alike and family members will usually stick up for one another, even if we don't always get along easily. In our story today we are going to meet some people in Jesus' family, at a tricky family meeting.

First, let's meet the family. (Give out speech bubbles to various children to read in turn.)

Mary Hello, I'm Mary. My oldest son is called Jesus. I'm very worried about him.

(Hold up a sign for all the children to read)

All Why are you worried about Jesus, Mary?

Mary Well, there are such big crowds of people with him all the time. Some of them have evil spirits. He makes them better, but some people say he's mad.

Jesus' brothers We are Jesus' brothers. We want to come and take Jesus home with us. It isn't safe to live like he is.

Jesus' sisters We are Jesus' sisters. It isn't normal to go round healing and teaching great crowds of people. He doesn't even have time to eat! We want to tell Jesus to come home and just be our brother again.

All But Jesus has very important work to do while he is on earth, you know.

Brothers But we are his FAMILY!

Thank the readers and explain that when Jesus' mother, brothers and sisters arrived at the house where Jesus was, they found it packed with people, all listening to Jesus. They couldn't get near him, so they told one of Jesus' disciples that they were there, and asked them to tell Jesus.

When Jesus was told that his mother, brothers and sisters had come to take him away home, he looked around at all the faces of the crowd. He could see that they all needed him. He knew he had important work to do with lots of people, and couldn't just live with his family. 'Do you know,' he said, 'who my family is? My family isn't just my mother, brothers and sisters, but every single person who is trying to live God's way.'

Jesus' family had to learn that although Jesus belonged to them in one way, he also belonged to everyone, because his work was to gather lots of people into the family of God.

Things to pray

Jesus, thank you for letting us
be part of your family.
We hope the family grows and grows
until everyone is living God's way.

Jesus' Friends

Things to read

James 2:14-24
John 15:9-17

Things to do

Do this, do that! The captain of the ship is given a suitable hat to wear, and everyone else is the crew, obeying the orders to make the ship sail well. (Possible orders: scrub the decks; climb the rigging; hoist the sail; lower the sail; drop anchor; weigh anchor; coil the ropes; everyone to port; everyone to starboard; all hands on deck.)

Talk about jobs where it's very important that people just do what they're told, and obey orders straightaway (such as soldiers and sailors, astronauts and fire fighters, and those working in an operating theatre). It doesn't matter whether they understand why they're doing it – as long as the person in charge knows.

When Jesus was talking to his disciples not long before he died, he told them that he wasn't going to call them servants any more, with him as their master. Instead he was calling them friends. What's the difference between being servants and being friends?

Collect their ideas in two columns on a sheet of paper, headed 'Servants' and 'Friends'.

Being friends of Jesus like this means that we'll be working with him on very important missions. There are things that Jesus needs done which only we can do! For instance, you may be the only friend of Jesus available to work with him in your classroom on your particular table, or in your playground. You are the only person who is right for a job of comforting someone in your family, or challenging the behaviour of someone who lives nearby.

Whatever jobs Jesus wants to work with us on, he will always give us the right training for it, the best opportunities and any special help we need. And we'll be working as a team, not with Jesus giving orders and us just doing it without understanding why.

So, if we want to be in God's team, we need to make sure we're keeping in touch with him all day long, asking his opinion and help, and not trying to go it alone. Jesus doesn't want us to work *for* him but *with* him.

Things to pray

Here I am, Jesus,
ready to work with you
for the coming of the kingdom.
What's our next mission together?

Hearing and Believing

Things to read

Ezekiel 2:1-5
Mark 6:1-13

Things to do

Sit in a circle so everyone is visible to everyone else. Choose someone present but don't let on who this is. Say, 'I'm thinking of someone who . . .', giving one clue at a time until the identity of the person has been guessed. The guesser carries on the game, until all the children who want to have had a go. With older children you could include some people who are in the church community.

The people we have been describing are well known to us. Some of them we have known since they or we were babies. We perhaps go to the same school. That's how the people of Nazareth felt about Jesus – how could he be so special? To them he was just the ordinary Jesus they had always known, whose mother's name was Mary and whose father was the town's carpenter. They knew his brothers and sisters. They were happy for Jesus to make their furniture or repair their houses, but they didn't want to think of him as someone special who could teach them God's thoughts.

And because they didn't want to hear, they found they couldn't understand what Jesus was talking about. (We sometimes block our ears if there's something we don't want to hear.) Read the children Mark 6:1-6.

That was in Jesus' home town. What happened in all the other villages and towns? All the people crowded round to listen to him because when they heard him they felt close to God, and that felt really good. Jesus knew he'd never be able to get round everywhere for everyone to hear him so he had a plan. How many disciples were there? Twelve. (Lay down twelve simple paper cut-outs of people as you say this.) Jesus split them into pairs (a child can do this), so how many pairs were there? Six.

He sent each pair of disciples out to the different villages and towns to preach to the people, encouraging them to change their hearts and their lives, to heal those who were ill and comfort those who were sad. (Spread the pairs out all over the floor.) And Jesus told them to go out just as they were, without money or luggage or insurance policies. They were to live simply and joyfully, and God would do the rest.

What do you think happened? There were still some who refused to listen, just as there are today. But lots and lots of people did listen to what they said, and turned back to God, and lots were healed.

Things to pray

Lord Jesus, help me to listen
with my heart as well as my ears.
Lord Jesus, speak into my thoughts and hopes,
my questions and my fears.
Amen.

The Spirit Comes

Things to read

Acts 2:1-17
John 15:26-27; 16:12-15

Things to do

Give each child a different coloured bunch of wool lengths. (For larger numbers of children make several groups.) With the bunch of wool provide a written message, reading it out to the child as you give it, and checking they know what it says. Now they all go round giving their message, and one length of their wool, to every other child. Here are the messages:

1. The disciples were waiting and praying.
2. Pentecost means fifty days after Passover.
3. Jesus had promised to send the Holy Spirit.
4. The Spirit sounded like a rushing wind.
5. The Spirit looked like flames of fire.

(Add to these or prune them as necessary for your group.)

Everyone should now have a bunch of different coloured wools. They lay these out in front of them. The children can now help you tell the story of Pentecost, by remembering the messages which went with each colour of wool.

Once everyone has added the bits of the story, pull it all together by reading the events as told direct from Acts, using a suitable translation. We have all been working together to tell the story today, and the Holy Spirit empowers us to work together with God and one another for good every day of our lives. What a lot of good can happen by seventy years' time if all of us work in the power of the Holy Spirit every day for the rest of our lives!

Things to pray

Come, Holy Spirit of God,
come to me and fill my life.
Let me live in your strength from now on,
and work with you
so that great good gets done!

Loving Obedience

Things to read

Isaiah 50:4-9a
John 14:21-24

Things to do

Dogs and owners. Everyone gets into pairs, and takes it in turns to be the dog and its owner at obedience classes. They are all directed to get their pet to walk to heel, sit, lie down, beg and stay. They are told to give lots of praise and encouragement to their pet as soon at it obeys the instruction.

Some of the children may have had experience of training a pet or watching working dogs, such as sheepdogs or police dogs. There always has to be a good friendship between the dog and its owner, so that the dog is obeying and working hard because it wants to please the owner it loves. How is that different from a dog who is badly treated and beaten? That just makes the dog crouch down frightened, or it might turn round and attack the owner. Real obedience is working together out of love. There are lots of stories of dogs who have done all kinds of brave and dangerous things, just because they love their owners.

Read Isaiah 50:4-5 from the Bible, preferably in a clear children's version, explaining that the prophet is talking about God's obedient Servant, who turned out to be Jesus. Jesus was obedient to everything the Father told him, not because he was scared of punishment, but because he loved his heavenly Father so much.

Things to pray

Father God, we want to obey you
because we love you,
and know that you love us.
Your loving kindness
is all around us in this world
and we choose to come to you and say,
'Let your will be done in us.'

True Greatness

Things to read

Philippians 2:1-11
Mark 9:30-37

Things to do

VIP spaghetti quiz. Have a pot with some different length pieces of string in it. Split the children into teams, and ask the questions. If a question is answered correctly, that team takes a piece of spaghetti. At the end of the quiz, each team ties its pieces of spaghetti together. The longest wins. Here are some ideas for questions:

1. Who is the Prime Minister of England?
2. Who is the Headteacher of (school)?
3. Who is the rector/minister/pastor of (church)?
4. Who is the captain of Liverpool?
5. Who is number one in the charts this week?
6. Who runs the Brownies here?
7. Who invented the telephone?
8. Which king had six wives?
9. Who plays (part) in (soap)?
10. Who introduces (animal programme)?

What makes some people important and famous? Talk this over, looking at such things as being rich, clever, good-looking, speaking for the rest of us, being specially bad or good. What about God – if he was to draw up a list of important people, would it look the same? What kind of things might God be more concerned with? You could remind them of what happened when Samuel was choosing a king from Jesse's sons – God didn't go for the tall, handsome ones but the youngest, in charge of the sheep. People look at the outward appearance, but God looks at the heart of a person.

One day some of Jesus' disciples were walking along the road having a bit of an argument. Was it about who had to do the washing-up? No. Was it about something Jesus had been teaching them? No. Was it about the road they needed to take? No. They were arguing about which of them ought to be the most important – the greatest of the disciples. Perhaps it went something like this. (Give out different 'scripts' to various children who can read.) Perhaps Peter was saying . . . (Peter reads out: 'I am best. I am very good at fishing. Jesus likes my fish.') Perhaps Andrew was saying . . . (Andrew reads out: 'I am best. I was one of the first to be called by Jesus.') Perhaps James was saying . . . (James reads out: 'I am best. My name starts with a J and so does Jesus.')

They all had their reasons for thinking they ought to be the greatest, most important disciple of all. That evening, Jesus asked them what they had been arguing about, and they all felt rather silly. It didn't seem to matter who was best when Jesus was there. But Jesus wanted to teach them something very important. And it's important for us to learn as well, because we are all Jesus' followers. Jesus explained that the way to be greatest in the kingdom of God was to be the last of all and the servant of all! Not richest, not best-looking, not sporting champion, but the last of all and the servant of all.

Things to pray

Lord, teach me the joy
of serving others for no reward
apart from knowing that I am making you happy.

True Religion

Things to read

Deuteronomy 4:1-2, 6
James 1:22-27
Mark 7:1-8

Things to do

Fix down a few sheets of paper to the floor and tell everyone they are in a land belonging to the great king. They can move around to the music but on no account are they to step on one of the sheets, as these belong to the king's enemy. Gradually add more sheets so that it becomes harder to walk freely. Anyone touching the king's enemy's land has to stay banished on that sheet, as they are now too 'unclean' to tread on the great king's land.

Talk together about some of the ritual rules we make, sometimes as games and sometimes for real, like not letting ourselves step on the cracks in the pavement, or stopping all the children playing with their toys by saying some special word, like 'Poop Nincom' (but they can when you reverse it and say 'Nincom Poop'!). Share any ritual rules the children have used. You could also read them A. A. Milne's poem about cracks in the pavement. Today we are looking at some rules which are worth keeping and some that aren't.

Remind them of the ten commandments given by God to Moses when the people of Israel had escaped from being slaves in Egypt. Basically, these ten commandments were all saying two main things: Love God and love one another. They were very good rules to keep and live by.

But over the years people had added all sorts of other ritual rules. To show you loved God, you kept yourself 'clean' by all sorts of rules like not touching dead bodies, not eating certain food, and never eating without a special washing ceremony that had to be done in exactly the right order. (What do they think God thought about those kind of rules? Would they really show that the people loved him? Or would they just show that the people had a lot of rules?)

Read from Mark 7, verses 1, 2 and 5. So Jesus, the Son of God, wasn't keeping all the little tiny rules as the religious leaders thought he ought to. When they picked him up on it, Jesus told them this: 'You think it's more important to follow your own rules than God's commandments! But it's God's commandments which are really important.'

(And what are God's commandments? To love God and to love one another.)

That's just as true for us as it was for them. We may have got ourselves clean and smart to come to church, because we want to show God he's important. But God's more interested in whether we've got ready to meet him by being kind and helpful this morning, whether we've been in touch with God at all by praying during the week, whether we're wanting to show off or not. Those things may not show on the outside, but they show up very clearly to God. The best-looking and the best-dressed people here as far as God is concerned, are those who are really trying to live the way of love.

Things to pray

Lord, I want to show my love and thanks
in the way I live my life.
I want everything I think, say and do
to be in line with your Law of love.
Lord, help me to be more concerned
with the state of my soul before you
than with my efforts to impress other people.
Amen.

Living Wisely

Things to read

Proverbs 9:1-12
Ephesians 5:15-20

Things to do

Tell or read a story which illustrates wisdom, such as the Emperor's new clothes, or the crowded house story, where a man complaining of his pokey home is advised by a wise man to get all kinds of animals to live in it with him. Then he is told to let them all go, and he ends up discovering how much space he has.

The child who spoke out and said the Emperor was really wearing no clothes at all was wise because he stuck with what he knew was real and true. The man who advised the farmer to fill his home up with animals and then have it to himself again was wise because he knew about people. He knew that we grumble when we want something we can't have, and that we're happy if what we have is better than what we used to have.

So we can be wise even if we don't get top marks for our spellings every week. We can be wise whether we are grown-up or still children. And sometimes children are a lot better at being wise than grown-ups! In fact, some of the wisest grown-ups are the ones who still go on thinking like children, still asking questions and marvelling at the world, still saying what they know is true.

As you can imagine, our great God is full of wisdom. That doesn't mean that he knows everything (although he does), but it means that God really understands why people act the way they do, and what makes each of us like we are. And because God is wise, he also knows the best way for things to happen. If we pray every day for God's will to be done on earth just as it is in heaven, then we can be sure that God will work with all the events of the day for good. He is so wise that he can even work with the bad things that happen, the arguments and fights, the disappointments and wrong choices people make.

(Place a large question mark on the floor.) If we are not at all sure how to put things right when we've made mistakes (place a cross over the question mark), our wise God can help us. (Place the question mark down again.) If we are bothered by things that are happening at school or at our club or at home (place the cross over the question mark), our wise God knows how to work in that place so that things are sorted out for good.

As God's children we are to live wisely as well. How do we do that? We need to go through life looking and listening. We need to seek God out every day. And we need to make good use of every opportunity we have for playing on God's team, fighting evil and working for good.

Things to pray

Jesus, did I hear you needed players on your team?
Well, here I am!
Did I hear you needed volunteers?
That's me!
I want to be on your side, Jesus,
fighting for good against evil,
fighting for justice and truth
with weapons of love and hope.
Who's for Jesus?
ME!

Trusting God in the Dark

Things to read Hebrews 11:8-10
Mark 8:31-38

Things to do Put some obstacles around. The children work in pairs, with one of each pair blindfolded. Their partner leads them carefully around the obstacles so that they don't bump into anything.

Point out that because we couldn't see clearly, we had to trust our partners to lead us safely through. If they had not been interested in helping us, they would have let us down. We trust those who we know are concerned for our safety because they like us.

Sometimes life can be fun and easy and we can see where we're going, and everything's working well for us at home, at school and with our friends. But at other times, it can feel as if we've got one of those blindfolds on; we can't see what to do for the best, and we don't understand where we are or where we're heading.

But God is never blindfolded or asleep, or too busy to bother with us, so he's the very best guide to trust; because he loves us he always wants the best for us and never lets us down.

Following Jesus doesn't mean that we shall never have any problems or bad days. But it does mean that even on the bad days, and even in the middle of all the problems, Jesus will be there guiding us through and helping us to cope well. God promised that he would do this, and he always keeps his word.

Things to pray Teach me, Lord, to trust you,
train me, Lord, to see
that even where the path is darkest
you are guiding me. Amen.

God and Creation

The Mystery of God

Things to read Isaiah 6:1-4
John 3:1-17

Things to do Bring in a lot of tight rolls of newspaper, thick enough to be firm. Work together to make them into an Eiffel Tower, using sticky tape to join the rolls together. They should find that the strongest shape to use is a triangle. If they aren't getting beyond the bendy stage, you can subtly suggest the use of triangles!

Draw their attention to the way triangles hold firm, and look at one to see why this is. All the way round, two hold the third in place.

Explain that today we are taking a look at what God is really like, and worshipping him. What do we know about God already? For a start, how many Gods are there? They may well mention lots of gods they have heard of. Agree that people through history have invented lots of gods, and anything we worship – including football stars and fashion – can be made into a kind of god by us. But we know that all these are pretend gods, which we make or think of ourselves.

There is only one true God and nobody invented God – God was already there; he always has been and always will be. That makes the one true God the only one worthy of our worship. And that's why we and our families make the effort to get up on a Sunday; we know that God is real and we come to worship him.

What is the only true God like? God is Father, the Creator (write 'Father' across the triangle), Son, our Saviour (write 'Jesus' in the same place), and Holy Spirit (write 'Holy Spirit' in the same place). We can't see the words clearly now because they are all one, and that's what God is like. If we also write the character of God round the edges (do this) we can see that the whole 'shape' of God is Father, Son and Holy Spirit all supporting and including each other.

That's why we call God a Trinity, or Tri-Unity – tri = 3 and unity = 1.

Things to pray

Glory be to the Father
and to the Son
and to the Holy Spirit,
as God WAS in the beginning
IS now
and SHALL BE for ever. Amen.

The Spirit of God

Things to read

Genesis 1:1-3
Acts 2:1-4
Mark 1:9-11

Things to do

Give out long strips of crêpe paper, or several sheets between a group, or use a parachute as the whole group. These things are waved in a way that expresses different moods, for example: angry, happy, gentle, excited, peaceful, wild, controlled, hopeful.

Share this poem:

> It's funny,
> my puppy knows just how I feel.
> When I'm happy he's yappy
> and squirms like an eel.
> When I'm grumpy he's slumpy
> and stays at my heel.
> It's funny,
> my puppy knows just how I feel.
>
> (Anon)

As humans we can feel all sorts of different things, and as God made us like him, and as Jesus showed us, we can tell that God also feels sad and happy, he's both peaceful and powerful, both gentle and strong. So the Spirit of God will show that too. Sometimes, like at the beginning of creation, we are told the Spirit of God was 'brooding over the face of the deep' (Genesis 1:2), full of love and hope for all that was going to be brought to life. (They can move their streamers like this, starting still, moving gently and then more powerfully.)

Or we can look at the time when Jesus was baptised. As they listen to the way Mark tells it, suggest they listen out for what mood the Spirit of God was in at this particular time. Use a clear translation to read today's Gospel; you may find it helps the children to have it projected on an OHP with a picture of water on an acetate behind it. Or have it written clearly on a blackboard with coloured chalks or on a length of wallpaper, with a 'watery' border drawn round it. Talk about the Spirit of God resting gently on Jesus, like a gentle white bird, and let them move the streamers to express this.

Everyone can read out together the words of God which Jesus heard as the Spirit rested on him.

Remind everyone of how the Spirit of God came at Pentecost (Acts 2:1-4), powerful and sounding like a great rushing wind and like fire. (Move the streamers or sheets like this.) The Spirit can come on all of us gently and powerfully, quietly or noisily. Sometimes the Spirit makes us feel suddenly very full of peace and calm, and other times it makes us feel full of excitement about Jesus and enthusiasm for following him no matter what.

Things to pray

Spirit of the living God,
I believe and trust in you,
and want to follow you all my life.
Come into my life and live there,
so that each day I may know you better
and love you more.
Amen.

Caring for Creation

Things to read

Genesis 1:24-31
Genesis 2:15, 18-20
Psalm 8

Things to do

Name the animal. Have a number of pictures of animals spread out on the floor or wall so everyone can see them. One person decides on an animal but doesn't say which it is. This person starts to describe the animal, one fact at a time, and the others try to guess which one it is. Whoever names it first has next go.

Explain that the Bible has included two versions of the story of how the world was made, one an even older story than the other. Show them the story we know best, the one at the very beginning of the Bible, with the world being made stage by stage, in six days, or ages. Adam and Eve – the first people – were made on day six, and they were told to look after the world.

Then read Genesis chapter 2. (Show them this.) This version of the creation story is even older than the other one. Both stories give us the same truth – that God made the world, and people, and gave them the responsibility of looking after it all. Remind them of Adam being taken around to name all the animals. What did he call the animal with long ears and a fluffy tail which hops about? What did he call the animal that is furry and striped, has sharp teeth and runs fast?

What the writer of the story is telling us is that, as human beings, we have the important, responsible job of taking good care of creation. How do they think we are doing? When do humans make a good job of looking after the world? Where do we mess up the job God has given us to do? On a sheet of paper or a blackboard, jot down their ideas in tick and cross columns. Talk through any ideas they have for ways we could do better, locally and inter-nationally. (Look, for instance, at recycling our litter, asking for simpler packaging, using feet and bikes and public transport more instead of cars.)

We have to look after one another as well – our friends and the people in our families. How? Again, share ideas.

Things to pray All good gifts around us
are sent from heaven above;
so thank the Lord, O thank the Lord,
for all his love!

God's Wonderful World

Things to read

Psalm 104:24-35
John 1:1-15

Things to do

Have a selection of earth's wonders to enjoy, such as bubbles that are so light that they float about in the air, things that sink and float, prisms that split the light into rainbows, and 'fly eye' lenses that split the world into repeated images, wine glasses of water through which images turn upside down, and spoons which give distorted and upturned reflections.

Gather around the objects once everyone has had time to experiment, and talk together about how the physical laws of our universe, which God has made, make these things happen, allow aeroplanes to fly, and let us stick safely on our planet without floating off into space. If you have a member of the congregation who is specially enthused by science, you could ask them along to join you, as you spend some time marvelling at it all. Whoever thought and loved all this into being, and keeps it going, must be amazingly wise, and different from anything we can imagine. He must be more than super-human, more than super-clever, more than super-imaginative. He must be outside time as we know it, as well as inside, and he must know all of us far better than we can ever know him. The name we give to this amazing great being is the Lord God Almighty, and he is so wonderful that we worship him.

Things to pray

Glory be to the Father
and to the Son
and to the Holy Spirit,
as God was in the beginning,
is NOW
and shall be for ever!

THE EVERLASTING KINGDOM

The Kingdom Grows

Things to read

Isaiah 55:10-11
1 Corinthians 3:4-9
Mark 4:26-34

Things to do

Bring a variety of leaves and have some reference books available so that they can be identified, together with their 'seeds'.

Talk about what has been discovered in the opening activity, and how small seeds grow into huge plants. Jesus loved using the world around us to help us understand spiritual things, and today we're going to hear how Jesus used growing seeds to explain spiritual truths for us.

First, he looked at the way seeds grow. (As you speak get a flower pot, fill it with earth and plant a seed in it.) Gardeners will talk about growing vegetables and flowers, but what do they actually do? They get the seeds and they put them in the earth. Then what happens? They water them and put them in a suitable place. Then what? Do they have to sit and watch all the time? Is it no more TV until the vegetables are ready? No, the seeds just grow, more or less on their own! They don't need the gardener to be there fussing over them every minute of the day. Wild plants don't have gardeners and they still manage to grow.

Jesus says that the kingdom of heaven grows rather like that. Just as we can look back and remember that we've grown taller over the last few years, and our knowledge of maths has grown, we've also been growing spiritually. We understand a bit more about who Jesus is now; we are getting more used to talking things over with God in our prayers; we are able to ask some of the big questions about what God is like and how the miracles happened. We are starting to think about what happens when people die, about right and wrong, about what it costs to be a follower of Jesus.

All this proves that the kingdom of God is growing in you, just as seeds grow in the earth. All that growing is God's doing.

There's another thing about seeds. They start off so small and can end up a huge plant. Jesus noticed that the mustard seed is specially good at that – it's one of the tiniest seeds (show some) and yet it can grow to the size of a tree, with lots of big, spreading branches where the birds love to come and shelter.

He said that the kingdom of heaven grows rather like a mustard seed. Explain that you're not going to tell them what that meant. What do they think he meant by that? (Talk over their ideas. The value of Jesus' parables was to get people thinking for themselves, rather than giving out the answers straightaway.)

Things to pray

Our Father in heaven,
let your kingdom come.
Let it come in me and my family.
Let it come in my school and my church.
All over the world, Father,
let your kingdom come.

(*Jesus, reign in me* can also be sung as a prayer today.)

The End of the World

Things to read

Psalm 46
Mark 13:1-8

Things to do

Predicting the weather. Beforehand prepare a large notebook with different types of weather pictures on each page. (The pages need to be thick enough for the pictures not to show through.) Everyone takes a turn in giving the weather forecast for the next day, and then you turn the page to reveal what it really is, and so on.

Predicting the weather in some countries is very simple because it's nearly always the same. In other climate zones, the weather is very changeable, which makes it hard to predict. Like the weather, some things in life are pretty certain, while others are things we have no idea about.

Today we're going to look at something which none of us knows much about at all, except that one day it will happen. It's the end of the world. We hear and read about all kinds of horror stories, where great chunks of meteors crash into the earth, or there's a nuclear war which kills all the people and the environment, or the sun suddenly flares up and swallows up earth. (Place down a few appropriate paperbacks and film fliers.)

Jesus helped his students (and us) to look at what the end of everything might really be like. He explained that there will be all kinds of terrible things going on beforehand, just as we read about in the newspapers and many poor people are having to live through at the moment – things like wars and rumours of wars, famines where many people starve because they have no food, and natural disasters like floods and earthquakes. (Place down appropriate pictures from newspapers and magazines.)

(Place down a cross with a question mark over it.) Do these things mean the end of everything is here? Jesus says they are like the 'birth pains' but they aren't the end (or the 'birth') itself. Jesus warns all his followers that we'll need to be on our guard, in case all the terrible things happening make us lose our faith in the God of love. (Cover the cross completely with the terrible pictures.) The ones who will be saved for ever are those who keep their faith (clear away the pictures so the cross is visible again) and have lived out their lives with love (place your hand on the cross), guiding others along the right pathways, and looking after those who need help. That was Jesus' way, and that is to be our way as his followers.

One thing we are sure about is that nothing which is loving, kind or true is going to ever disappear, because God will gather it all up safely. That means that the people who are kind and loving and honest will be heroes and heroines at the end of time, whether they are rich or poor, famous or completely unknown in this world. All goodness gets a hero's welcome!

Things to pray

Lead me, Father, through this life,
along the pathway of your love.
May I keep to it, help others to find it, and,
one day, may it lead me straight into your heaven!

The Saints in Heaven

Things to read

Isaiah 25:6-9
Revelation 22:1-5
John 14:1-6

Things to do

Pass the halo. Use a shampoo shield and put on some music. Pass the halo round. The one wearing it when the music stops is out, folding their arms in the circle to show this. Carry on till only one or two are left and give them a small prize.

Describe a picture to the children and ask them to imagine it. Then show them the picture. It's always quite hard to describe something so that we know exactly what it's like. Sometimes it's better to describe what it feels like than what it looks like. Someone could try describing what it feels like to be lost and then found again. Someone else could try describing what it feels like to be really tired after a hard match and come home to a shower and your favourite meal.

Today we are celebrating all the saints who have lived and struggled through this life, just as we are now, and they were such close friends of Jesus that he was able to do amazing work through them. When they died and came into the presence of God, it must have been a little like coming home to a hot shower and our favourite meal after a long, hard match. They were given a great welcome in heaven, like a wonderful homecoming. We're going to listen to some people describing it.

Put on some quiet, gentle music and read Isaiah 25:6-9, Revelation 22:1-5, and John 14:1-6.

Today we are thanking God for the way these people lived. Now they cheer us on as we walk through our lifetimes, as Jesus' friends. And one day, we hope to join that great party in heaven!

Things to pray

You spread a banquet for me
in the presence of my enemies;
my head you have anointed with oil
and my cup is overflowing.
Surely goodness and kindness shall follow me
all the days of my life,
and I shall live in the house of the Lord for ever.
(From Psalm 23)

The Eternal King

Things to read

Daniel 7:9-10, 13-14
Revelation 1:4b-8
John 18:33-37

Things to do

Sit in a circle and share some of the dreams we remember.

Give each child their sheet on which they can draw Daniel's dream as you read it to them. Can they work out who the 'son of man' is that Daniel saw in his vision? Explain that, as with all dreams, it's picture language. So why a throne? Why fire? They show us God's great power, and fire also purifies gold and silver, brings light into darkness and has to be treated with great respect.

What kind of king is Jesus shown to be in this dream? He's the King of all time and space, not for a little while but for ever.

Just before Jesus was crucified he was taken to Pilate, the Roman governor, who wanted to ask Jesus about him being accused of being a king. Was it true? Have the Gospel written out as a script, with two people reading it.

Yes, Jesus was a King, but he didn't have earthly power like Pilate, for instance. How was it different? Jesus reigns in people's hearts and souls. Our lives become his kingdom's territory when we invite Jesus into them. You can tell a life where Jesus reigns. The person is gradually growing wiser and more loving, finding it easier to forgive, and they find they are wanting to reach out to others and do good. Perhaps they have already begun to notice some of these things happening in their own lives.

Things to pray

Our Father in heaven,
hallowed be your name.
Let your kingdom come;
let your will be done on earth
as it is in heaven.
Give us today our daily bread
and forgive us our sins
as we forgive those who sin against us.
And lead us not into temptation
but deliver us from evil.
For the kingdom, the power and the glory are yours
for ever and ever. Amen.

Index of Uses

TOPICS

Advent	8, 12, 24, 25, 26, 27
Alive	56, 58
Anger	52, 53
Anoint	50
Baptism	27, 80
Believe	66
Bethlehem	25, 28, 31
Blind	38
Bread	20, 46
Bridge	16
Calm	45, 81
Change	26
Christmas	9, 11, 28
Conservation	82
Cost	54
Creation	80, 82, 84
Cross	54, 88, 89
Darkness	14, 76
Day	42
Deaf	36
Death	54, 88, 90
Disaster	88
Dog	69, 80
Doubt	58, 66
Dream	91
Family	62
Fear	45, 56
Feeding 5000	20, 46
Feelings	80
Food	20, 46, 47
Forgiveness	34
Friends	64
Future	88
Gifts	31
Greatness	70
Grow	17, 86, 87
Healing	34, 36, 38, 43
Hear	36, 66
Heaven	16, 90
Holy Spirit	68, 78, 80
Homeless	43
Jerusalem	50, 52
Journey	30, 43
King	8, 9, 28, 30, 50, 72, 91
Kingdom	40, 41, 51, 71, 86, 87, 91
Life	20, 21, 56
Light	14
Love	54, 69, 73, 89
Mountain	48
Messiah	12, 13, 26, 50, 51
Nazareth	66
Obey	64, 69
Palm Sunday	50
Pentecost	68, 80
Prayer	52, 73, 74, 75
Religion	72
Rescue	18
Rich	40, 70
Rules	72
Saints	90
Sea	44, 45
Servant	64, 69
Sheep	18, 28
Shepherd	18, 28
Signs/symbols	34, 42, 50
Storm	44, 45
Suffering	54, 55, 88
Temple	8, 9, 52
Ten Commandments	72
Time	42
Transfiguration	48
Trinity	78
Trust	76
Vine	17
Wash	27
Water	27, 32
Wedding	32
Wine	32
Wisdom	74
Word	11, 12
Work	64

BIBLE CHARACTERS

Adam and Eve	82
Andrew	71
Bartimaeus	38
Daniel	91
David	8, 9, 28, 50
Deaf man	36
Gabriel	9
Herod	30
James	48, 70
Jesse	70
John	48
John the Baptist	26, 27
Joseph	9, 28, 42
Mary	9, 28, 62
Moses	72
Nathan	8, 9
Peter	48, 70
Philip	46
Pilate	91
Prophets	12, 13, 25
Rich young man	40
Samuel	70
Thomas	58
Twelve disciples	66
Wise men	30

ACTIVITIES

Acting a part	28, 38, 40, 56, 58, 62, 68, 70
Action song	46
Blindfold games	38, 76
Climb a mountain	48
Creeping in the dark	14
Dogs and owners	69
Don't step on a sheet	72
'Do this, do that!'	64
Dreams	91
Dressing up	28, 40
Forfeits	54
'Get ready to…	24
Growing a vine	17
Guess the object	12
Guess who	66
Happy families	62
Imagine	48
'I went to wedding…'	32
Jigsaw meals	20
'King David says…'	28
Lion hunt	56
Musical instruments	36
Name the animal	82
Newspaper bridge	16
Newspaper Eiffel Tower	78
Observation	84
Obstacles	76
'One day I would love to go to…'	30
Parachute	80
Pass the halo	90
Pass the ring	8
Peas and water	52
Pictionary	11
Prediciting the weather	88
Procession	50
'Simon says…'	34
Sing	46, 49, 51
Sound effects	28, 32, 34, 44
Spinning a tray	54
To the rescue	18
Try again	58
VIP spaghetti quiz	70
What's different?	26

BIBLE REFERENCES

Genesis 1:1-3	80
Genesis 1:24-31	82
Genesis 2:15, 18-20	82
Genesis 28:10-17	16
Exodus 16:2-4, 9-15	20
Exodus 24:9-18	48
Deuteronomy 4:1-2, 6	72
1 Samuel 16:1-13	50
2 Samuel 7:1-11, 16	8
2 Kings 4:42-44	46

96 Index of Uses

Psalm 23	18	Luke 1:26-38	8
Psalm 46	88	Luke 2:8-20	28
Psalm 51:1-17	34	Luke 4:16-21	12
Psalm 78:70-72	28	Luke 24:36b-48	56
Psalm 104:24-35	84	John 1:1-5, 9-14	11
Psalm 107:23-32	44	John 1:1-15	84
Proverbs 9:1-12	74	John 1:43-51	16
Isaiah 6:1-4	78	John 2:1-11	32
Isaiah 9:6-7	24	John 3:1-17	78
Isaiah 25:6-9	90	John 3:18-21	14
Isaiah 29:17-21	36	John 6:1-15	46
Isaiah 40:1-5	26	John 6:24-35	20
Isaiah 42:5-7	38	John 10:11-16	18
Isaiah 43:25	34	John 12:20-33	54
Isaiah 50:4-9a	69	John 14:1-6	90
Isaiah 55:10-11	86	John 14:21-24	69
Isaiah 56:6-8	52	John 15:1-8	17
Isaiah 60:1-6	30	John 15:9-17	64
Isaiah 61:1-2	42	John 15:26-27	68
Isaiah 61:1-4, 8-11	12	John 16:12-15	68
Ezekiel 2:1-5	66	John 18:33-37	91
Daniel 7:9-10, 13-14	91	John 20:19-29	58
Zechariah 9:9	50	Acts 2:1-4	80
Matthew 2:1-12	30	Acts 2:1-17	68
Mark 1:1-8	26	Acts 2:22-24, 36-38	56
Mark 1:9-11	80	Romans 8:28-30	62
Mark 2:1-12	34	1 Corinthians 3:4-9	86
Mark 3:20-35	62	Galatians 5:22-25	17
Mark 4:26-34	86	Ephesians 5:8-14	14
Mark 4:35-41	44	Ephesians 5:15-20	74
Mark 6:1-13	66	Philippians 2:1-11	70
Mark 6:30-34, 53-56	42	Hebrews 1:1-3	11
Mark 7:1-8	72	Hebrews 11:8-10	76
Mark 7:31-37	36	James 1:22-27	72
Mark 8:31-38	76	James 2:14-24	64
Mark 9:2-9	48	1 Peter 2:21-25	54
Mark 9:30-37	70	1 John 1:1-4	58
Mark 10:17-31	40	Revelation 1:4b-8	91
Mark 10:46-52	38	Revelation 12:1-5a	14
Mark 11:1-11	50	Revelation 19:5-9	32
Mark 11:15-19	52	Revelation 22:1-5	90
Mark 13:1-8	88		
Mark 13:24-27, 32-37	24		